the sound of red

Also by Brenda Saunders

Firestick (Mayn Press)
Looking for Bullin Bullin (Hybrid Press)

Brenda Saunders

the sound of red

Acknowledgements

Many of the poems in this collection have been published in the following journals, websites, newspapers and anthologies:

Australian Poetry Anthology, Australian Poetry Journals, Blue Giraffe Press, *Canberra Times*, *Cordite*, *dotdotdash magazine*, eurekastreet.com, *foam:e*, *Famous Reporter*, *Five Bells*, *Mascara Literary Review*, Melbourne University Press, Meuse Press, *New Writer Magazine*, *Pixel Paper*, Poetica Christi Press, *Poetrix*, *Rampike Magazine*, styluspoetryjournal.com and *Wet Ink*.

'Living with De Chirico' was awarded the NSW Society of Women Writers Prize 2008 and 'Looking for Bullin Bullin' was awarded second place in the 2011 David Unaipon Manuscript Prize, Queensland Premier's Literary Awards.

Special thanks are due to Deb Westbury at the Varuna Writers' House, Carolyn Gerrish and members of the Round Table Poets for their support and invaluable criticism.

the sound of red
ISBN 978 1 74027 799 0
Copyright © Brenda Saunders 2013

First published 2013
Reprinted 2017

GINNINDERRA PRESS
PO Box 3461 Port Adelaide 5015
www.ginninderrapress.com.au

Contents

Night train	11
Rothko in Hamburg	12
Spin	13
The Art of Travel	15
Point de vu	16
L'Arc de Ciel	17
Rhapsody	18
Le Jour de Muguet	20
Melancholy	21
The sound of red	22
Illusion	23
Miniature	25
Configuration	26
Hotels	27
Muzeum	33
Griefswalden: East Berlin 2008	35
Promised land	37
Living with de Chirico	38
Goya	39
Inside Edward Hopper	40
Aphrodite	41
Last bell	43
The Bridge	45
Book of Hours	46
Impressions	47
Art options	48
Kafka's table	51
The world inside	52
Distance	54
Gate of the Moon	55

The Well	56
La nuit blanche	57
Third age	58
Moving on	59
Fashion statement	60
Calling	61
Nu-ku	66
Shortcuts	67
The shadowed world	71
Reinventing the landscape	75

'Poetry is not pastel covered but blood red and black'
– Gwyneth Lewis

Night train

Border check, midnight
Saisoniers
stamp cold ennui
down the corridors
Caps, blank faces
the flick of a match
Chiaroscuro

At Delft, a hoar frost
freezes land to sky
Breughel figures
cross a field
Ink drops on a
winding page
of snow

Roof lines, fences
crisscross
a black on white
abstraction
Mondrian
in the window
of the train

Rothko in Hamburg

'Take one step back from the wall, absorb the colour field at full stretch – note the synthesis of opposites.' – Mark Rothko

How many blues are riding
under the swish of a brush?
Lightly dipped, juicy turpentine
floods a sky, light as Turner's
on *Varnishing day*.
Violet tingles at the horizon.
There's a scent of lavender.
Specks of oil expand, free-falling
on currents of air.
Wings ruffle the edges. Aqua
washes in with the tide.
A triangle plays the breeze.

I read the guide, ready to leap.

       Someone up close is asking

    Was machen Sie?

I step back
a few paces.
Rectangle
blank wall
settle back
into place.

Spin

'I give voice to the longing for immateriality' – Jean Tinguely

The city is grey. A border town of concrete and granite wrought from some glacial rift. Stone flagging set with precision and skill. A stillness stretches over the Rhine: factory smoke freezes in mid-air.

This is Basel.

There is disorder in the old town, satiric gusto on the Theaterplatz.
Absurdist fountains fling and spit in senseless play. Junk-sculpture on parade.

> Clanging hammers beat
> a chime in mock discord
> Town clocks tick dismay

The anarchist brings parody to his native town.

Near Paris in a forest haunt, a Cyclops inspects the canopy. Inside a scrap-iron staircase leads to pandemonium: fantastic memories of childhood in the Schwarzswald.

> Recycled steel
> recasts the hollow man
> with an open mind

In the New World a tower of junk revolves in useless frenzy. Motorised spin becomes a culture statement.

> Man-made rejects
> a city's detritus
> set on self-destruct

In the bonfire heat
art as prophesy screams
L'Homage to New York

Jean Tinguely (1925–91): French-Swiss kinetic artist and committed socialist. *L'Homage to New York* was his motorised self-destructing junk-sculpture.

The Art of Travel

'Grand Tour of Europe' – Cosmos Tours 2008

I am running through
a Rousseau forest
Eyes flicker under leaves
Night shades
A troika speeds
through frozen air
Pine needles bristle
There is no moon
just a Nolde sunset
sinking below
a wash of mauve
Navy blurs the edges

>   Someone on the coach
>   is complaining
>
>   about the trees

We've left the autoroute
taken a back road. Soon
they'll turn on the lights
and black out the view
from my picture window.
They'll turn the heating up
add a touch of Strauss
to lull us into a dozy sleep
until we get to Budapest
or is it Bucharest?

Point de vu

At the villa Clemente
the *pensione* is full
I sleep in the conservatoire
Madame's jewel hand
waves to a dome of glass
Ah   Nice   such art

A small moon breaks in

In Rousseau's jungle
wildlife is immutable
only the eyes stir

Life-sized *Women*
in the garden at Nice
step through mauve shadows
A filigree of trees
mottles sun on balconies
Figures of Bonnard

Matisse looks down
on the rue du Paradis
paints his salon red
A flamenco line
draws arabesques on chairs
Rings of southern light

Dufy couples
promenade under tall palms
a wash of blue

the Mediterranean everywhere

L'Arc de Ciel

Feisal's new villa overlooks the lake at Geneva. A vista of grey surrounds the Jet de l'eau. We've come to decorate, transfigure the salon into a Neo-Bedouin world of *trompe l'oeil*. Clouds drift in an azure dome, gold twinkles the chandeliers. Marble swirls the floor in a sand drift. With sponges and paint, we create an endless faux desert. Curtains ruffle like flaps on an Arabian tent (the affectation of a Paris designer). The prince holds court on Persian carpets, sits with men in robes, discussing the real estate spread out below. Looks for a mirage of sunshine above the city mists.

Rhapsody

'The viewer is encouraged to experience the sublime potential of nature, understanding that the scene should be perceived and idealised by a human.' – Caspar David Friedrich

It is open season for hunters
now. Antelope stand alert
Gunshots caught
in a circle of sound

A stag leads the herd
high up, to pastures
– sunshine on pines
close to the snowline

At the rim of the world
he holds ground. On his head
he carries boned trees
shaped by the wind

*

We came upon them grazing
at the end of summer
– a 'sylvan' detail from some
half-remembered painting

Our eyes are unused to vistas
Views of mountains dissolving
in mist, the void tilting
beneath unsteady feet

We come from the plains
where skies sit on a line of heat
– distance and space measured
on roads leading to the sea

*

Overnight snowfalls signal
an early winter, the reality
of the herd exposed. Ready
to return into frozen shadows

We take the easy road down
follow signs to the village
Locals are wary of strangers
with questions, foreign accents

Tourists taking the small train
through the Val de Travers
Looking for 'wonder'. Romance
Landscapes close to the sublime

Le Jour de Muguet

'Struck down by Death at the moment of glory' – epigraph, Amedeo Modigliani 1884–1920, Pierre Lachaise Cemetery, Paris

I find him lying at the feet of the bourgeoisie, under a slab.
Cramped between rows of imposing statues. Family shrines.
Candles lit for men who never took a firestick into the dark

or sparked a wild idea when the world outside spun in chaos.
His dying star, fallen too soon, rises brightly as a point fixed
in legend: draws the world here to read his epithet.

They leave a sprig of *le muguet* for love: see his Art and Life
as romance played out as tragedy: living portraits stacked
against walls of indifference. Breathless under the weight.

Melancholy

Closed-in, the long white lung is sighing. Panic echoes along a curve of heaving air. On and on anxiety stretches toward the shifting light, a way out beyond the muffled breathing. A heart flutters against windows that have already rusted tight. Weighed down with the intricacies of lead. Hope has seized up here under pressure. Above, my ribs line up like roof struts, thick as trees, bolted together they hold in loss. Once this space welcomed the air, exhaled fresh ideas riding high. Now, melancholy drifts at their soft edges. Waiting to take the next breath.

The sound of red

'We are cluttered with images and only abstract art can bring us on the threshold of the divine' – Mark Rothko

Lit from above eight dense and brooding panels
rise from the floor, subdue the circling walls
A triptych folds cool to warm in infinite variations
of a fugue: rosin glints on burnt sienna
manganese showers a residual turbulence
Notes of an evening raga settle the dust
Indian red lifts from a funeral pyre
From low banks our captive gaze settles
to night vision, distils the neutrality of grey
Eyelids flicker a blink of stars. Dark energy
From indigo depths a *missa solemnis*
carries the slow breath of solace

Illusion

In Mantua a tower sways above the plain: from the massive parapets you can see as far as Switzerland.

Inside the Palazzo Ducale, a classic stairway leads to rooms of state: Renaissance grandeur moulding civic pride.

> Each stone worn thin
> by centuries of footsteps
> raising patronage
>
> A thousand scabbards
> pockmark winding frescoes
> Snow on verdant fields

In airy rooms, Gonzaga's entourage parade life in the *Reggia* – on borrowed time.

> *Buon fresco*
> renders vanity and power
> in *tableau vivant*
>
> Rich brocades
> dissolve in clouds of white
> *il restauro*

Life-sized figures stroll through an orange-grove: fresh dew on the grass.

> Deep vistas extend
> perspective in the room.
> Painted escape
>
> In real time
> open windows
> duplicate mists of blue

Around the walls of *la pittura granda*, a cardinal, a prince, his wife and his hounds step on faux marble. A dome of stars posed in celestial union.

> Silent intrigue
> wedded to ducal largesse
> The averted gaze
>
> An errant foot
> slips from the painted stage
> Mantegna winks

Miniature

Dragon clouds curl a gold leaf sky.
A brush of fine hair paints a beard
details a guardsman with his bow
fine tipped arrows at his side.
On tapered pins Chinese horses
pick their way, carry musicians
across a sheet of painted snow.
A blast of horns announce
the Emperor on his elephant.

Configuration

Ghery turns the idea of building on its head. Bends art and technology to his will. Anything is possible. With silver card and sticky tape he frees the form of a giant fish, leaping to the Bay of Biscay. His scales ripple on titanium plates, shimmer the river running by. Narrow streets meet at the square open to sunlight. Echoes soar inside the shell, walls spiral to a nautilus.

*

In a Spanish foundry, Sierra reshapes raw iron into serpentine coils, installs his waves in the Guggenheim at Bilboa. Up close one tap rings tight. Metal presses in, holds the smell of dense matter. Salt air works the surface to a patina brushed with rust: flaking like a tanker left for scrap. Corrosion in slow time. From high above, coils float light as streamers tossed on a calm sea.

Frank Ghery: architect, Guggenheim Museum, Bilbao, Spain
Richard Sierra: sculptor, *The Matter of Time*, installation, Guggenheim Museum, 2008

Hotels

Amsterdam

Behind the canal four walls meet in a square court three floors down: a breathing space at the back of our hotel. A breeze skirts off my windows, billowing gauze waiting for spring. The courtyard is three floors below. The sun hasn't reached there yet. I am watching a man with a bronze pate on the floor below. He leans out clutching the iron grille beneath his window. A girl across from him smokes, standing in the yellow light between velvet curtains. She is watching an old woman dressed for church (I forgot it was Sunday). Her face sinks into a well of shadow. They are watching a woman planting bulbs in a window box. Her laughter lifts the cold patches of grey like sunlight after rain.

Two Women in a Courtyard, Delft, Pieter de Hooch, 1657–60

Neuchâtel

The Hotel du Lac looks down on restaurants. Beside the new marina they have built an artificial park. I remember tall reeds, wading out naked from the tiny beach. Now there are pebbles. Sharp boulders keep the grass in place. On this rare summer day people sit or lie stretching the pale sunlight. Some have come for a picnic. Others look around, shed clothes self-consciously baring their whiteness to a new sensation: warm air on flesh, body pressed against grass. Skin used to the dark rub of clothes. Mountains. The weight of snow.

Luncheon on the Grass, Eduard Manet, oil on canvas, 1863, Musee d'Orsay, Paris

Stopover Pucin

Rising heat in the room has sent me to the panelled window. I try to lean out but it's sealed off. I feel the ice pressing against the glass outside, measure the distance from the tenth floor; the time it would take to drop from here to there. I remember the grappling hook I saw last night, the steely life-line in plaited cord, well hidden under the curtains: wondered who it was for. I am ready to jump through this pre-dawn image, drift like snow in a wash of Nippon blue. But the bathroom offers an escape to cool-sense water, definition in black and white tiles. The welcome tick of plumbing in the sub-strata under the bath.

Landscape in the Snow, Japanese scroll painting, Maruama Okyo, 1784. Nippon blue: Sea of Japan (also a brand of paint)

East Berlin

I arrive late on the Alexanderplatz. The Park Inn cuts a block from the Berlin sky. At Reception the sign reads 'Wait here for the next Smile'. American know-how will take the East into a new deal. I am given a room, the mirror image of the one in Rome, only the décor has changed from terra rosa to business grey. On the square the fountain stands erect, like a fifties candelabra: the cascade ignored by the listless youth strolling below. Everything is in a state of flux. Shops in the American Mall stand empty. New recruits, the young and the daring, pass by Starbucks, gape at the Gehry ceiling. So much bling!

Universal city, photomontage, Georg Grosz, Berlin, 1922
Frank Gehry: postmodern American architect

Montmartre

It is spring in the Rue de Cadet. On the top floor my roof slopes, so I walk side on across the room. My dormer windows open to a view of rooftops. Blue slate crowds the hill to Pigalle. At the end of the street the Folies Bergère is quiet, closed for the day. At night the sign flashes neon red. Doors open to the Grand Foyer lit by candelabras. Resplendent in faux metal, the ponies prance, their manes a fling of gold. Tourists wait for the nine o'clock show, looking for the risqué in *Gai Paris*. I think of Josephine Baker, sashay across the sky, singing 'Bye-bye blackbird'.

Rehearsals at the Folies Bergère, Toulouse Lautrec, lithoghraph, 1895

Toledo

Autumn is not the season for tourists. There is no view from the room, only a wall darkening with age. A laneway leads to the hotel kitchens and the scent of marzipan. I could be anywhere, except the men are yelling in their local Spanish. I can hear people on the cobbles in front, running downhill as the rain hits. Another storm circles the town, isolated on the plain of Castile. We pass the Alcazár on the way to the Roman bridge. I have roamed the Jewish Quarter searching for El Greco's Museum, only to find it closed. I believe the best paintings are now in city museums, far from here.

Toledo in a Storm, El Greco, oil on canvas, 1600–10, Metropolitan Museum, New York

Muzeum

'Day 6. This afternoon includes a sightseeing tour of the Auschwitz Concentration Camps, a chilling reminder of the Holocaust. Evening in beautiful Krakow.' – Grand Tour of Europe, Cosmos Tours 2005

Coaches line up in the parking bays
tourists processed at the gate
have fact sheets on the 'history'

An original staircase in sterile white
leads to restrooms underground
Renovations, 'camp heritage' style

Sealed units in blood-red tiles
A bare globe in the ceiling
the hiss of air piping through.

A school group scream and punch
laugh off the lesson for the day
on the steps of the crematorium.

On their way out they pack up close
line-up for the photo opportunities
beneath *Arbeit macht frei*.

Along the road, free enterprise
expands to compromise.
Langerhaüsen convert to living space.

*

Arbeit macht frei: Work sets you free
Die Langerhaüsen: storehouses

At Birkenau a flat chill hits the air
sharpens wires on the perimeter
wraps the camp in tight

Gates stand open for guided tours
Dark huts line on the lawn
Open for Inspection.

The mercury drops down railtracks
gleams on *Reichbahn* lines
Trains on the hour to Auschwitz

Warm air in the Guardsroom
lightens *der Schmertwelt*.
Posters of Warsaw burning.

Tourists crowd for postcards
insignia of the Third Reich
Replicas forged in iron.

Everywhere a blanket greenness
spreads: each mound and pit worn
to a level footnote on the grass.

die Reichbahn: Third Reich railway system
der Schmertzwelt: ills of the world

Griefswalden: East Berlin 2008

The hotel is run by theatre people
adjusting to post-Stasi life
Signed photos line the Frustuckzimmer
>Posters of Afro-Americans
>>– jazz men on tour
>Cabarets in the Emmanuel Kirke

Frau Leichner plays Kommissar
directing the show –

> *Take the No 4 down Griefswalden*
> *Right side*
>> *Alexanderplatz*
>> *Der Amerikan Mall*
>> *Starbucks*
>>> *– some like*

> *Look for Lust*
> *Get down*
> *Follow the Spree*
> *The DGR ist unterground*

She takes the map, laughs
stabs her ruby finger at a broken line.

> *Heir, heir, heir ist der wall*
> *– everyone like*

She never mentions the West

*

I find the Spree: follow her dotted line
to the island Muzeum
On the steps outside, an artist confronts
the phantom wall: leaves his message
Niemer mehr – Never Again
along an empty street

Promised land

We have built a wall long enough
to paste the pages of our history
– details of old betrayals
Drawn a line to mark the truce
with a barricade of concrete

Olive groves stand on a land divided
their branches always in shadow

We had already seen the signs
watched fault lines split
at every checkpoint
– cracks in the phantom shield
held up to guard our future

Human traffic walled in
along a dead-end street

Belief forged from the desert
will never yield under fire

On both sides, our young lie buried
in shrouds. We build ghettoes
with stones from other conflicts
Pray for peace in different tongues
to a different idea of God

Living with de Chirico

The clock on the piazza has stopped at four
Caught in the light, alien figures stand apart
poised for action. Set pieces in a scenario
mystery played out in striking discord.
Faceless people look to a sun already lost
in a darkening sky, in the luminous threat
of an impending storm. Are they waiting
for change: a new life to open doorways
lead them to a reality offstage?

*

A girl draws in the stillness, the chill
at the end of an autumn day. City blocks
hold off her fear of distance. Lost in the
anonymity of the street, she's ready to find
her true direction. Turning, she catches
her mirror image in the window frame.
Acts out her idea of Rihanna. Dreams
of video clips. Photographs her ideal self
talking to nobody on her mobile phone.

*

On Sunday afternoons words sharpen
at the edge of balconies, closing in.
Rising voices glance off a column
ricochet off steel chairs. Heels scrape
a square of sunlight. Terrazzo glitters.
White heat hits a pane of frosted glass.
A sliding door cuts out the summer gale.
Muffled thunder breaks somewhere.
Inside, conflict folds in the dividing wall.

Goya

Works across the walls of his country retreat. Moves quickly behind shuttered windows. Oily pigments wipe out the leafy world beneath: frescoes from a gentler time. Panoramas sink beneath raging skies. He watches the silent demons rise. In *The House of the Deaf Man*, day and night are one.

Dragged to the surface
the underside of magic
rises black on black.

Revolution spreads
on a wide-loaded brush.
Rebellion crowds in.

Cannons vibrate
at his sooty fingertips.
A sky back-lit by fire.

A swipe of ochre turns
a cheek. Anger rides
on a touch of carmine.

Caught in the spotlight
white impasto captures
a cringe of fear

Screaming at heaven
his pilgrims trail their faith
lost on a winding hill.

Pitturas Negras.
A nation's grief on display
in the Prado.

Inside Edward Hopper

Room in New York

We are in the front room upstairs. Just your usual rented brownstone. Apart from the piano. We only came to look at art and now we're inside a painting, held by the dark frame of the window at night. He's not talking to me. He's posing, pretending to read, stretching the paper into black and white shapes. I tinkle a few notes. Waiting. Electric light can be so brittle. It sharpens the space between us. My red dress has become the focal point in the picture, flesh tones soft against mahogany. Some guy is watching from the apartment across the street. He thinks I haven't noticed. I should pull the drapes, block out his angle of vision. But then we'd never get out.

Nighthawk

There's no stopping him: he went off in the middle of the night. Said he was going out for cigarettes. I'm not in this picture. There's no door, so I don't know if I could get in. Or how he will get out! He's sitting in there smoking, watching the couple at the counter, well the redhead anyway. The waiter is making small talk. Passing time. They are all shaped in a diner window. Separate, like extras in a movie. Artificial light freezes the frame, draining the colour. He's always looking for the story beyond the painted surface. But this time he's gone too far.

Paintings by Edward Hopper: *Room in New York,* 1932; *Nighthawk,* 1942

Aphrodite

Come home with me to Paphos
and I will show you love, he said.
So we stood on line of cliffs
watching the surf break below.

See how her shawls have turned
to rock. Thrown back they mark
the birth of a goddess rising.
She draws the tide, breathes love
into life. Sets her will on course
speeding to mortal hearts
far from the Aegean.

*

Later, we find her carved in relief
On a throne, sea and foam cling,
cloth falls as she springs into life.
This Greek has captured
Aphrodite's joy, rendered
her legacy onto marble.
Cold to the touch.

*

Another *Head of Venus* sits despondent
on a plinth, her face a detail of perfection.
Her body lost to plunder. In Paris she
steps from her garments. Commanding
attention, she waits to be worshipped.
Beneath her smoothness, fame and beauty
stir the world to jealousy and rage.

*

I see her everywhere in Paphos streets.
In a shop close to our hotel, she leans forward
offers fruit. I see only a golden pomegranate.
The proud tilt of her head. She carries beauty
with her, coils of hair above a creamy neck.
Like me, she has no need for worship.
Pedestals. High ideals beyond her reach.

Last bell

Glaube, Hoffnung, Liebe: faith, hope and love

The biplane is a 'found object'
weighed down by history.
Poppy stalks lie caught
between furled wings
– seeds in paper kites
poised for take-off.

Nearby the propeller shaft
lies in a wad of concrete.
The blades no longer spin
on their silver helix.
Glaube, Hoffnung, Liebe
– ash on wasted fields.

What alchemy has wrought this from the fire?
Sent rasping embers questioning the air?

Too late for answers
from yesterday's men
seizing the skies
for love of country.
Belief –
the last refuge of war.

Die Volkszählung: Census

In a room open to the air
the books are stacked by number.
Rain will not wash away dates
or names of those missing
in the battle (records
treasured by the Reich).

Details etched on metal leaves
survive the fire – immutable
as secrets of the Stasi.
Soft as winding scrolls
these sheets will bind
the lives of strangers.

What of the stubble dried
and pressed in the codex?
Are seeds a sign of renewal?
Imagination driven
on the wind, scatters
the wisdom of burnt books.

On the last bell, each note strikes
Deeper. Fear is a low thud
running through the feet
of the people. They search
for promised rain. Flowers
Das Lied von der Erde.

Mohn und Gedachtniss: *Poppy seeds and Remembrance*, Anselm Kiefer, installation, 2006, Contemporary Art Museum, Berlin

The Bridge

Art and life are anchored here
weighed by this broken bridge.
There is no plumb line to check
the cement steps tilting towards us.
Led to the edge we hover
between earth and sky

A smoky tableau on a far wall
lifts the eye to wild poppies
In the dust pinpoints of colour
scrape through the concrete rubble.
On the dizzying horizon
Hope falls into focus.

from Anselm Keifer, *Erdlebenbilder: Earthscapes*, installation, Art Gallery of NSW, 2010

Book of Hours

Across the pages monks illuminate
stories from the seasons of the year.
The cycle of men's lives, the labour
of their days. Each parchment gleams
with colours richer than life. Summer
harvests, the smell of grapes ripe
on the vine. Holy wine blessed
to celebrate the festivals of saints.

Winter brings a cobalt sky, a canopy
of Heaven pricked with stars.
Snow on the fields. Cattle in barns
watch the Christ child below. Angels
pluck music from the spheres. Lutes
fine tune our senses to the Sweetness.
Quills curling on sheets, draw in
the hours on the calendar of life.

The Sweetness: Medieval concept that emerges from the total sensory experience of a painting

Impressions

We'd seen the prints in art books
– black and white scaled down
to postcard size. Occasionally
a Rembrandt face loomed from
the shadows, Renoir's dots
reduced to tones; a Monet pond
framed in an A4 page

We recognised each artist by
titles and dates. Imagination
never stretched to meet a work
in actual size, until Monet's pools
filled the Musée L'Orangerie.
Life-sized *Nympheas* under trees
reflecting ponds at Giverny

Beauty and fame have launched
his prints far from Paris walls.
Snow domes flutter his petals.
Lilypads tint Dior umbrellas,
blur the image of an artist
painting for years. Searching
for a true sense of light on water

Orangerie: Musée de l'Orangerie, Paris

Art options

I thought I'd add a dash of colour to my day, look to new horizons. But instead I've painted myself into a corner, can't see beyond the square. I wanted closure, but now I've got my face to the wall, my vision out of focus. As I draw the curtains on the past, a window of opportunity opens up new perspectives. From where I'm standing it's a blank canvas there for the taking. Turning a new page I sketch a broad plan in black and white, outline the shape of things to come, my vision for the future. I've already pencilled in a profile for the way ahead. But a few areas need my detailed attention. Drawing up new models will mean smudging a few figures. Not one to be kept in the dark, I'll block out the negative, brush off any shades of grey, look to New Pathways Going forward. After all with a stretch of the imagination, a line drawn in the sand can lead to the light on the hill. There are endless possibilities in the frame as I re-shape the big picture.

Kafka's table

'It is not necessary to leave the house. Remain at your table and listen. Do not even listen, only wait…be wholly still and alone. The world will present itself to you for unmasking, it can do no other…'
– Franz Kafka

The places you find

I've collected ideas, tucked them up my sleeve. Memories too are stored, firmly pleated. Like an accordion, rhymes and rhythms wait in the folds. Random thoughts lie scattered. If they slip out at night, I'll be alert to collect them. Stuffed in deep spaces they'll be hard to resurrect. Ribbons of words are rolled up in bands. Pinned together, they catch on my fingertips, the long ones find their place on a line. Hyphens wait for me to fit them in, commas fade away. Reflections spill out of their wrapper, work their way to the top. Ready for the poet to call them up.

The places that find you

These are the quietest spaces: they offer more than oblivion. Time is the fast train speeding by, measuring distance point to point. Step off and solitude is waiting there. These moments come unannounced. Each pause seems like a year. Time and space are together on this. Places of reflection are still and silent they lead into unguarded territory, to enchantment or possible revelation. Somewhere between sleep and waking fear will seek you out, draw you in close. Live in the long moment between everything and nothing. The imagined places are always there, waiting to find you.

The world inside

The weather here is known to change
At the edge of summer warm air
drops swiftly to chill. Oak trees
brighten a sky stiff with cold

My room has windows curving
to catch each scrap of sunlight
A blackbird calls in high resolution
back-lit by cloud floating in

I sit at my writer's table. Call up
the world inside my head. Rooms
with a different view –

too wide to hold
deep enough to fall into

*

I watch the people stamping flakes
from their boots, smell the loaves
baking at the Boulangerie à la Côte
Frozen air through the open pane

And the view downhill takes me
past rows of vines spread on a
stiffened sheet. Reeds at the lake
clump like straw packed in snow

White tails from planes crisscross
the blue. The Alps break through
in a landscape of their own
Sunlight. Mountains of ice

too wide to hold

*

Patonga is the end of every journey
The road winding in from nowhere
stops at a shack on a stretch of sand
The slow creek sinking with the tide

Small boats blink red to green
Fishermen call over velvet water
There's a hum of traffic far off
A glow from the wakeful city

The river was lost long ago, the sea
coming in to drown the valleys
Hills lie back folded like breasts
Eucalypts cling to a shoreline

deep enough to fall into

Distance

You write me letters

stretch the faint edge
of words
in a spidery hand

say you need me
closer
to catch

my meaning

*

You say
you think of me

when a north wind blows
over the Alps

I hear ocean currents
reshaping the shore line

between us

Gate of the Moon

to Nora Krouk

The old man commands the silence
tap-tapping his closed in years.
Long days of forgetfulness
sharp moments caught on a word.
With steady voice he calls up worlds
that seem as close as yesterday.

Tuned his ear his wife sings
of a life past. Recalls stories, family
she's never met. Images of travel.
A homeland they'd never found.
Summer nights, the scent of Harbin
Chinese bells at the Gate of the Moon.

Reading her lips he breathes in
epic journeys. Safe returns.

The Well

Love is the echo
of a stone falling
the rising pail.

In drier years
the well sinks deeper
no one sees.

When love has gone
hauling the rope
makes heavy work.

La nuit blanche

Your last sigh leaves behind
a sudden weight of sadness
pressed against my skin.

White nights close in the fear.
Wakeful thoughts in slow time
brighter than the moon.

Rooms hold the life that was
that might or should have been.
Memories crowd the corners.

Days pass when I tighten old habits
hold myself together, step outside
a lifetime planned for two.

At the quiet edge of loneliness
there is space for new ideas.

la nuit blanche: 'white night', or insomnia

Third age

Sometimes I'm lost
as words spin off
free fall.

Thoughts implode
into black holes.

Light years zoom
– the past
a flash of nebulae.

With nature on rewind
I'm tempted to press

eject

Moving on

Dreaming of trains
the insomniac
upstairs
rides an exercise bike

*

On our stationary bus
T-shirt in front says
'I'm moving
in the fast lane'

*

Anxious girls
text their friends
– check the action
on Facebook

*

Young men in Audis
cruise the market
– scan mobiles
for the state of play

*

A three-legged dog
scooters up the street
knows
where he's going

Fashion statement

I'm a *One-off*. A *Pin-up* at the high end of haute. My elan gathers the adventurous, adjusts the unpredictable: that *je ne sais quoi*! I'm quality svelte, hot off the press. Shaped and swathed, I thread my way with seamless artistry, purring down the catwalk of history. Of course I'm biased! If cut on the cross, I'm bound to unravel. At times I'm taken down a size, let down, stitched up. Still I hold it all together. When pinched and tucked I suffer pins and needles. End up a caste-off on the cutting room floor. Destined for the rack, I'd rather be hung with *Armani* (he says in five languages how *froufrou* is my *frisson*, how chic my couture) than pegged as synthetic *Esprit*. It's not that I've got tickets on myself, but *Label* is everything. I could be sized up for *Ready to Wear*, phased out in *Ping Pong After 8*. Still, better a *Country Road* in beige, than *one-size-fits-all* in the bargain basement.

Calling

I know a woman
who rang to say
she was blown
away

leaves her story
on the message
machine

I hear the wind
tossing her
through

the small holes
in my phone

*

Some man
rings to say

I'm off today!

a stranger out there

somewhere
waiting

for a wrong number
to call
him back

*

I know a girl
who packs
her stuff

rings
to hear me say
the things
she knows

will make her stay

*

I know a man
who says
he's over me

rings me up
from who knows
where

just to hear my voice
telling him

I've gone
somewhere

*

The operator
says

Hold the line
then
I'm putting you through

threads my voice
along a wire
of thin air

*

Some person calls
who never speaks

leaves slow breaths
on tape

my thoughts
running
across space

to catch
their meaning

*

I hear a man
asking
in a voice
I do not know

Where are you?

His question
played back
too late
to be
somewhere

*

They ring me
often

ask for aid

in a moment
between empathy
and fear

I hear the needy

crowding near

*

I know a woman
who never
takes her calls

plays them
back

sometimes
to empty walls

Nu-ku

Summer

> A single note
> stretches the evening
> the lonely koel
>
> On the floral clock
> day turns around
> rows of dying blooms
>
> Velvet furls
> dark canopies
> night cry of bats

Winter

> From the train
> footsteps on snow
> A Chinese scroll
>
> Figure skaters
> on sheet ice
> turn a new page
>
> Like a feather
> falling on snow
> I let go loss

Shortcuts

In tidy towns
trees never touch

On the road map to peace
repairs are ongoing.

Each morning
swallow one fear
with the *News in Brief*

Trees in drowned valleys
remember the hill

On the train
commuters pack in
the working day

Poetry the poor relation
brings a feast to the wake.

The shadowed world

Two views of Brett Whiteley

This face is moon-like, spread
in mottled dots. Software
pinpricks his eyes, darkens
one cheek to his favourite shade
of blue. Yellow cap, a flower
behind the ear: a signature
salute to his sixties youth

A mask emerges, luminous
One side flashes red to green
Holding the light it signals
stop or go to wild moods
swinging out of focus
Layers of perception
blur at the edges

Where is the Brett we saw
in these multiples of one
the man we thought we knew?
The shock of the new!
A Sydney's child: quixotic imp
of the liquid line, painting
the harbour into view.

The Cage

People fear the fireball spinning towards them.
Is this 'collateral damage' or a shooting star
flung out of orbit? Escape hovers
at the edge of the unknown.
Caught in the searchlight
they flee the present danger.

There is no time to think of freedom.
Somewhere along the way they lose
the details of their lives.
Forget the meaning of belonging
– collect a new self from scraps
caught on the cyclone wire.

Mandala

The rim of the sun pulls tight
against the fading sky
Pieces break off and sink
into oily blackness.

Only the island remains
spare and bleak: a wasteland
lost to fire, drifting
in a pool of acid rain.

Too late now for meditation
a mantra ringing the earth
or one last insight to save
a dying planet.

Sleepwalker

She slips from the space between dream and sleep: finds her way to the window. Familiar objects fade away as she drifts, lost in a wash of viridian. She steps to the edge of the painting. Up close the jade mountain is cool to her touch. She moves through caves, floating barefoot on crystal. At the far side, she sees the Glass Mountains, finds horizons silver in the light. Landscapes rolling forever in the humid night.

Laurence Daws: *The Promised Land* Exhibition, S.H. Irvine Gallery, Sydney, 2011

Reinventing the landscape

'Fred Williams was able to conceptualise the landscape from an aerial perspective…his notations painted over golden grounds, which he described as painter's honey…'

'…he sees the world in terms of colour' –

At *Werribee* a fire holds the ridge, shimmers gold.
It spreads along the cliff, smokes the sky in a heat-haze.
Gums shrink to vibrant specks of chrome. Etched deep
in dry point the gorge shadows a river in drought.

In changing weather his space dissolves into streams.
Broad stokes swirl the river into flood. Pools stir up
a cloudy slurry. Viewed from above his branches
fall loose as twigs carried on a current.

At the falls there is no water, just a blaze of cadmium
Raging. Tilted up, the plants appear to fall back
sink into the ground. A 'foul bite' cracks the ravine.
Dark as umber, stones hold the heat, blacken the terrain.

'…in sensuous touches of paint' –

We've learnt to read his symbols. Each stroke of oil
a finger intimate to the touch. Dots shape a line
of grasses, a slab of colour rounds a tree.
His blunt canvas soothed with 'painter's honey

In his *Landscape with trees*, I would trace the outline
of his verticals, track the reach of sentinel gums
beyond the frame, smooth the edge of a trunk.
The sun filtered on eucalypts soaring to the light.

Search the gully for textures lifting from tree ferns.
Rocky outcrops embossed in patterned shadow.
My fingers sense the weight of paint, thick on the brush.
Find touches of colour falling on leaves from the canopy.

'…tilting the landscape' –

The plane flies low over a curve of ochre-country.
Tree stumps tilt at a slow angle, their branches rising
to meet us. Boulders scatter, a waterhole stretches
on the horizon, framed in a triangle of sky.

Fred paints the Pilbara from above, watches the way
rock crumbles into dust. Trees flash, a dull tint
signals mulgas on a hump of ore. Claypans turn blue
in a wash of rain. New life flickers in the shallows.

Below us the perspective tips. A mine falls into focus.
He paints the man-made hills, raw earth blowing
from ore tailings. Sees the beauty in change
Scars on the landscape. Signs of renewal.

'…with the random scatter of objects' –

I move through rooms of golden summers, smell the sun
in scumbled oils. A patch of yellow becomes a sway
of native grasses. Across a field his stunted bushes
hold the horizon against the white heat of the sky.

If I could reach out, I would follow the fence line
finger my way through a patch of scrub. Rows of acacias
in scabby dots, the stumps of trees felled after a fire.
Feel charcoal under my nails, bush crackling as I pass.

Quotations from 'Fred Williams: Infinite Horizons', curatorial essay,
Deborah Hart, National Gallery of Australia, 2011

www.ingramcontent.com/pod-product-compliance
Lightning Source LLC
Chambersburg PA
CBHW062151100526
44589CB00014B/1781